Old and New

Paul Humphrey and Alex Ramsay

Illustrated by
Sarah Young

This old doll is made of china.

Some new toy cars have batteries to make them work.

Old cars look very different from cars today.

These houses are over 100 years old. The buildings behind them are very new.

People's faces change as they get older.

People wore very different clothes when Grandpa was a boy.

Oak trees can live for hundreds of years.

Bikes are painted much brighter colours today.

New push-chairs have tiny wheels.
Old prams had big wheels.

Old leaves are brown and brittle.
New ones are green.

Some of the things on this page are old and some are new. Can you tell which ones are which?